A PLANET CHOKING ON WASTE

UNDERSTANDING GLOBAL ISSUES

Published by Smart Apple Media
1980 Lookout Drive
North Mankato, Minnesota 56003
USA

This book is based on *A Planet Choking on Waste*

Library of Congress Cataloging-in-Publication Data

A planet choking on waste / edited by Jill Foran.
p. cm. -- (Understanding global issues)
Includes index.
Summary: Explores the problem of refuse, from common litter to toxic waste, on a global scale, covering the environmental, social, and economic implications of waste disposal.
ISBN 1-58340-165-2 (hardcover: alk. paper)
1. Refuse and refuse disposal--Juvenile literature. [1. Refuse and refuse disposal.] I. Foran, Jill. II. Series.
TD792 .P58 2002
363.72'8--dc21

2001008447

Printed in Malaysia
2 4 6 8 9 7 5 3 1

EDITOR Jared Keen
TEXT ADAPTATION Jill Foran
PHOTO RESEARCHER Gayle Murdoff
COPY EDITOR Jennifer Nault
DESIGNER Terry Paulhus

Contents

KG-89-SH
NL
EN LOMMER

Introduction

People and industries in developed countries generate billions of tons of waste every year. From common litter such as bottles and cans to toxic materials such as paint and cleaning chemicals, the world is gradually becoming overburdened by waste. The average amount of household garbage generated in the developed world is about 1,100 pounds (500 kg) per person per year. Although this is an alarming figure, it is nothing compared to the enormous volume of waste generated by the world's many industrial processes. Industrial waste is not always readily apparent. Materials such as sewage **sludge**, mining spoils, construction debris, and contaminated water often escape the common definition of "waste." Still, they account for a large percentage of what cannot be easily reused and therefore must be disposed of.

Today, humankind is more wasteful than ever. Most people in rich, developed countries buy all kinds of products and then throw them away without thinking. This behavior not only adds to the piles of waste that are produced every year but also contributes to the depletion of Earth's natural resources. In an effort to keep up with consumer demand, industries waste huge amounts of natural resources. Forests are cut down to supply materials for construction and manufacturing, and fossil fuels, such as coal, oil, and natural gas, are used to provide energy for many industries. Fossil fuels have developed over millions of years from the remains of once-living organisms. Earth has only a limited supply of these resources, and yet they are used in abundance to power all sorts of industrial processes. In fact, the average industrial process uses just 10 percent of the raw materials originally fed into production. A typical power plant wastes 65 percent of its energy input, and a car wastes about 90 percent of the energy in its fuel tank. Vast quantities of usable materials, along with enormous quantities of used materials, are thrown away every day.

Because so much waste is generated on a day-to-day basis, disposal has become a major problem. Traditionally, most developed and developing countries have disposed of waste by dumping it into large pits called landfills, or by burning it in **incinerators**. These methods of dealing with waste seem convenient because they provide easy solutions for keeping large amounts of garbage out of sight and out of mind. These methods of removal are not perfect, though. Many countries are running out of space for landfills, and many more are concerned that incineration causes too much air pollution.

As garbage continues to accumulate throughout most of the world, governments are finally beginning to move away from dumping or burning waste, and they are moving toward reducing and recycling waste. In most developed countries, people can recycle by collecting paper, bottles, cans, and plastics, which are then broken down and made into new products. This helps to conserve Earth's limited resources, and it reduces the amount of waste that must be dumped or burned. The problem of waste disposal is not simple, but it becomes easier to solve when individuals and industries work to reduce the amount of waste they produce.

A car wastes about 90 percent of the energy in its fuel tank.

There are more than 170 million cars in the United States and nearly 400 million in the world. Fortunately, automobiles are the most recycled consumer product.

Choking on Waste

Garbage is nothing new. People around the world have been producing and disposing of waste for thousands of years. For most of our history, much of the waste created by humans has been recycled by nature. People have developed their own systems of waste disposal through the ages. In Norway, scientists recently uncovered an enormous mound identified as a Stone Age garbage dump. Early peoples in the area created this dump to rid their living spaces of refuse. Ancient Greeks and Romans developed waste disposal methods as well, including out-of-city dumps and elaborate sewer systems.

In the Middle Ages, these ancient systems of garbage removal were forgotten. At that time, the most popular answer to dealing with waste was to throw

In 2001, the city of Buenos Aires, Argentina, collected nearly 5.5 million tons (5 million t) of municipal solid waste.

it out the window. This waste was largely organic, which means that it was composed of natural materials. As a result, it was gradually dispersed into the environment by the natural processes of decay. Unfortunately, while decomposing on the streets, these piles of garbage hosted a variety of germs, insects, and vermin, which then led to outbreaks of disease. It was not until scientists produced convincing evidence of the link between dirt and disease that societies began once more to see the importance of clearing away waste.

While some scientific discoveries have helped to re-establish systems of waste management, other achievements in science have led to an increase in waste production. New inventions paved the way for the Industrial Revolution. This period, which began in the late 18th century, changed the nature of production by replacing manual labor with machines. Goods that were traditionally created by hand were now being manufactured in vast quantities in factories. One consequence of the Industrial Revolution was an increase in society's demand for a variety of goods. As a result, the volume of waste began to grow significantly throughout Europe and North America.

Waste production skyrocketed in the 20th century. This was due mostly to the growing consumption of products by people in developed countries. New goods, including plastic and chemical products, were invented in order to meet growing market demands. The creation of such artificial substances made waste disposal a much more serious problem. Not only did the volume of waste increase substantially throughout the 1900s, the "new" garbage of the 20th century was not all biodegradable. This meant that it could not be recycled naturally or removed easily. As economic demands continued to increase in the late 20th century, the volume of waste in developed countries grew to alarming proportions. By the late 1990s, solid waste production in developed countries had reached more than 10 billion tons (9 billion t) per year.

A recent study by the National Safety Council estimates that more than 63 million personal computers will be discarded by 2005.

Today, the amount of waste continues to pile up. People are

generating waste faster than nature can break it down. As well, industries are still producing many materials that cannot be broken down by nature at all. Consumers in developed countries are becoming increasingly demanding, and industries are working to meet their demands. The ever-increasing production of so-called disposable goods, such as razors, pens, and diapers, will only subside when consumers stop buying these products. In the meantime, manufacturers continue to invent more convenient products to suit the growing number of people living hectic lifestyles.

The processes of manufacturing also generate great amounts of waste. For example, the manufacture of an average car produces about 16 tons (15 t) of solid waste and large amounts of wastewater. A single gold ring may involve the

The automobile industry consumes more copper, glass, zinc, leather, plastic, lead, and platinum than any other industry in the U.S.

displacement of about three tons (2.5 t) of material in mining and processing. In addition, nuclear power has created waste **byproducts** that are so hazardous they must be isolated for thousands of years. Every day, countless industrial processes create huge amounts of harmful wastes while depleting the world's limited natural resources.

It is estimated that the volume of natural resources required to support industrial society is 50 to 90 tons (45–85 t) of material per person per year. Some of the world's richest countries have caused environmental damage by depleting natural resources outside of their borders and by exporting hazardous wastes to poorer countries. Yet many of these countries, including Japan and the United States, are also leaders in the development of new technologies designed to reduce the environmental impact of waste materials. Many of these new technologies are aiming to develop **closed-loop systems** that reflect natural recycling processes.

The United States could save millions of barrels of oil each year if oil used in automobiles and industrial processes were recycled.

Nature operates with a closed-loop system, recovering and recycling Earth's materials. Since the Industrial Revolution, humankind has "broken the loop" by creating huge amounts of non-recyclable waste. The goal of a **sustainable society** cannot be achieved with disposable "one-time-use" products. A sustainable society is also unlikely to succeed when production systems waste 90 percent of their raw materials. The aim of all industries should be to mimic nature by developing closed-loop systems that eliminate waste altogether. Unless industrial society can learn to adopt the closed-loop principle, the **biosphere**—without which we cannot live—will eventually be ruined.

KEY CONCEPTS

Closed-loop systems and a sustainable future Nature's closed-loop system consists of cyclical processes in which Earth's materials are reused on a continual basis. Examples of this system include the water cycle, the renewal of the atmosphere, and the decay of vegetable and animal waste to enrich soil. As part of the closed-loop system, nature recycles biodegradable waste, which is made of substances that will decay naturally. The waste will then break down into elements that help to nourish soil. The invention of artificial goods has hindered the natural systems of decay and renewal. Many new products are non-biodegradable, which means that nature cannot break them down. This factor, together with the misuse of natural resources, threatens the future sustainability of the environment. To achieve sustainability, humankind must make use of natural resources without harming the closed-loop processes that are so vital to the health of the environment.

All Kinds of Waste

Waste comes in many forms, ranging from household garbage to spent nuclear fuel. Each type of waste presents different problems. While some simply carry germs or unpleasant odors, others pose serious threats to human and animal health. Most waste is either **inert** or **putrescible**. Inert waste consists of matter that does not decay. Materials such as glass bottles, bricks, and concrete are all inert.

Waste comes in many forms, ranging from household garbage to spent nuclear fuel.

Putrescible waste consists of plant or animal matter that is capable of being decomposed by microorganisms. Items such as paper, cardboard, food scraps, and grass clippings are all putrescible garbage. Although careful management of most inert and putrescible garbage is required, neither form of waste is very harmful.

Waste is generated through a variety of processes and in a number of modern-day settings. Municipal solid waste is the most obvious example of modern waste. It is composed of items that people in households, restaurants, and offices put into their garbage cans. About 30 to 60 percent of the trash contained in municipal solid waste is putrescible and can be composted. Composting is

In many developing countries, less than 75 percent of household waste is transported to landfills. Large amounts of waste are often left uncollected.

Estimates indicate that as much as 40 percent of landfill material comes from the construction and demolition of buildings.

an easy and responsible way to manage some forms of household waste. Items such as rotting vegetable peels, eggshells, leaves, and paper can be gathered together and placed outside in a pile. The trash in the pile will gradually decompose into a rich substance called compost, which can then be used to fertilize gardens or farmland.

While composting is an effective way to manage some household garbage, most municipal solid waste also contains materials that cannot decompose, as well as toxic items, such as batteries, cleaning fluids, and paints. The mixture of putrescible trash with non-biodegradable and toxic materials restricts the processes of natural decay. In some countries, governments have asked citizens to separate their household waste into categories so that garbage can be easily composted and recycled. Still, only one in three people take the time to separate their waste, even in countries where there are legal penalties for not doing so.

The world's largest quantities of waste are produced by agriculture, construction, and mining. Agricultural waste includes matter such as crop residues and manure. In many cases, these types of wastes can simply be plowed back into the soil. This type of recycling is becoming more difficult, though. Increasing populations and consumer demand have made farming very competitive. Small family farms have been replaced with large corporate farms that use modern equipment and **intensive** growing methods. This has resulted in amounts of manure and crop residue that are too large to be recycled or reused.

The recycling of construction-related waste also presents frequent problems. Construction waste includes

WASTE FACTS

Between 30 and 60 percent of household waste can be composted.

Each year, the average U.S. family throws away the paper equivalent of seven trees.

About 25 percent of household waste is in the form of packaging.

In the U.S., more than 2.5 million bottles are thrown away every hour.

demolition debris and damaged or unused building materials. Although it is largely inert, the weight and variety of construction waste often makes it awkward to dispose of or recycle.

Mining activities create the largest amounts of solid waste. Spoils from mining consist of excavation materials known as **gangue** and waste residues known as tailings. Mining waste tends to be disposed of close to mines. In some countries, mining companies are now required by law to clean up their waste. Before these laws came into effect, mining companies did not have to follow such rules. Heaps of ugly, sometimes toxic, waste were left behind once these mines had closed down. Some mining operations in developing countries continue to pollute land and water. For example, a gold mine in Irian Jaya, Indonesia, generates more than 40 million tons (36 million t) of waste each year. This waste contaminates surrounding rainforest, threatening various plant and animal species.

In some countries, mining companies are required to clean up their waste.

Although mining generates some toxic materials, it is the world's numerous industrial processes that create the largest quantities of hazardous waste. Metal works, chemical plants, paper-making factories, food-processing plants, and many other manufacturing operations produce all sorts of toxic waste. In fact, the developed world creates about 440 million tons (400 million t) of hazardous waste each year. Some of this waste becomes non-hazardous through biological processes,

The Cape Flats Wastewater Treatment Facility in Cape Town, South Africa, has the capacity to treat 53 million gallons (200 million L) per day.

but much of it builds up and remains highly toxic for hundreds or even thousands of years. The developed world also contributes to the generation of another type of waste—sewage sludge. Sewage sludge is formed by the treatment of wastewater, which is generated by both industrial processes and domestic sources. Wastewater consists of things that go down the drain, such as human waste, chemicals from household cleaners, dirty dishwater, and various industrial wastes. Wastewater is treated at sewage treatment plants and then dumped into nearby rivers or oceans. For centuries, most sewage was left untreated and was simply piped into the nearest body of water. Today, large quantities of untreated sewage still flow into rivers and oceans worldwide, polluting coastal waters and damaging marine life.

Few countries in the world publish accurate statistics on waste. However, a report published by the Organization for Economic Cooperation and Development (OECD) in the 1990s estimated that developed countries produce an annual amount of 460 million tons (420 million t) of municipal waste, 1.6 billion tons (1.5 billion t) of industrial waste, and 8 billion tons (7 billion t) of other wastes, including agricultural refuse, mining spoils, demolition debris, and sewage sludge.

Until recently, most non-recyclable waste has been generated in developed countries. However, in the last two decades, industrialization has spread into the developing world. Countries such as China and India, as well as many countries in Southeast Asia and Latin America, are experiencing rapid economic growth. As a result of this growth, there have been substantial increases in worldwide waste production. Large areas of previously undamaged land have been subjected to road building, intensive farming, mining, and construction. This means that developing countries have joined richer countries in producing and disposing of vast quantities of construction debris, sewage sludge, power plant ash, and mine tailings. Wastes from industrial processes and consumer goods are on the rise in developing countries, too.

The people who live at the "Smoky Mountain" landfill in Manila, Philippines, earn about $4 per day scavenging garbage.

PRINCIPAL TYPES OF WASTE

Municipal Solid Waste This type of waste generally consists of the everyday garbage that is thrown out in households, offices, and small businesses and then is taken away by municipal garbage collectors.

Wastewater Wastewater can consist of industrial waste, human waste, and runoff from rainwater. In the developed world, there are now strict rules concerning the release of contaminated water into the environment.

Agricultural Waste This waste generally consists of crop residues and animal droppings. Slurry is also an agricultural waste. It consists of fine particles of manure mixed with other farm residues. Slurry, along with farm residues derived from chemical spraying, often contaminates local groundwater.

Construction Waste This waste consists mostly of debris from demolished buildings and unused or damaged construction materials. Few countries have controls or laws concerning the disposal of construction waste.

Mining Waste Mining activities produce several forms of waste. Excavation produces residues of mineral ore and non-ore material known as gangue. The separation of metallic ore produces waste residue known as tailings. Wastewater is also produced in high quantities and is often released into rivers without proper treatment.

Industrial Waste Industrial waste is derived from industrial processes such as manufacturing.

Sewage Sludge This type of waste is generated by the treatment of wastewater, either from domestic or industrial sources. Domestic sewage is made up of whatever people flush down the toilet or wash down the sink. Industrial sewage consists of wastewater of widely different consistencies and levels of harmfulness.

Gaseous Emissions Waste emissions include a wide variety of gases, such as carbon dioxide, methane, sulfur dioxide, nitrous oxides, and carbon monoxide.

City Recycling Coordinator

Duties: Prepares educational programs, manages contract negotiations for the collection of recyclables, evaluates facilities involved in recycling
Education: Bachelor of science degree
Interests: Environmental issues, such as waste management

Surf to the Office of Solid Waste's Web site at www.epa.gov/epaoswer/osw/mission.htm for information about related careers. Also visit www.collegeview. com/career/careersearch/job_profiles/envirocon/rc.html for more information about recycling coordinators.

Careers in Focus

Most recycling coordinators begin their careers in related positions in small cities. The success of the programs in which they work often determines their future job prospects.

A major part of a recycling coordinator's duties involves managing recycling programs. Recycling coordinators are responsible for developing strategies for citywide recycling. This might include scheduling pickups and deliveries to recycling depots as well as negotiating contracts with trucking companies that specialize in hauling recyclables.

Recycling coordinators are active within the community. When they are not visiting recycling depots, they are involved in preparing educational programs for children and adults. Educational programs create awareness of the need to recycle. They also teach people ways in which they can reduce the amount of waste they produce.

On the technical side, recycling coordinators perform periodic checks of recycling facilities. They evaluate contamination levels, recycling rates, and collection amounts. This information helps them develop new recycling plans or restructure existing ones.

Recycling coordinators often go on to senior-level positions in waste management or policy development.

Hazardous Waste

Wastes are considered hazardous to people or the environment if they are toxic, poisonous, explosive, corrosive, flammable, or infectious. Although many companies may not directly generate harmful wastes, they are likely to use products that were created by other companies that do. Thousands of harmful substances are in use around the world, and many more are created every year. Because of consumer demand, more than 80,000 new chemicals go on the market each year. Traces of these chemicals travel long distances in air and water, causing damage everywhere from the Arctic to the Amazon.

International guidelines on the management of hazardous waste were first introduced in the mid-1980s. At that time, developed nations were routinely shipping toxic materials to the poorer developing countries because the costs of disposal were lower, and regulations for dumping were non-existent. Today, there are laws in place to regulate the exportation of harmful wastes. International law on hazardous waste is centered on the United Nations' Basel Convention. The aim of this convention is to control the movement of hazardous waste across borders. The convention also prevents the illegal transfer of waste and provides assistance for the management of hazardous materials.

By July 2001, 148 countries had joined the Basel Convention. The list of participants did not include the United States, which, on its own, creates one-third of the world's hazardous waste. The U.S. did not join the convention

People who work with hazardous waste must wear protective suits made from chemical-resistant substances.

because of disagreement over which wastes should be defined as hazardous. Countries often disagree about definitions and classifications of waste. However, those belonging to the Basel Convention have agreed to a long list of materials that should be considered hazardous. The list includes countless wastes produced by everyday industrial activities such as motor manufacturing, chemical engineering, and power generation.

Countries participating in the Basel Convention also agree that hazardous waste should not be moved across borders unless the importing country is willing to receive it. Countries exporting the waste must also be satisfied that proper disposal arrangements are available. Despite this agreement, cross-border trade—both legal and illegal—continues on a large scale. As well, hazardous substances outlawed in the West are still vigorously marketed in the developing world. In order to maintain human and environmental health, stricter regulations must be placed on the creation and trade of hazardous materials worldwide.

Nearly 440 million tons (400 million t) of hazardous waste are produced globally every year. Of this total, the U.S. generates more than 30 percent.

KEY CONCEPTS

Hazardous waste Although biological processes quickly break down most hazardous wastes, some can remain toxic for years. These hazardous wastes are known as persistent organic pollutants (POPs). Not only do most POPs disrupt **ecosystems**, they also accumulate in fatty tissue, making them very dangerous to animal and human health. POPs remain in the environment for a long time, resisting decay and traveling very long distances on currents of air or water, or by other means. Negotiations are underway for an international treaty banning the production and use of the most dangerous POPs.

Nuclear Waste

Less than 0.1 percent of the world's waste is generated by the nuclear industry. However, that small amount of nuclear waste probably causes more concern than all other wastes put together. The production of nuclear power is a controversial issue. Nuclear fuel is much cleaner than fossil fuels, such as coal, oil, or gas. Compared to the burning of fossil fuels to create electricity, nuclear power generation produces very little waste. Also, nuclear fuel can be reused or reprocessed, providing a source of energy for centuries after fossil fuels have been used up. Because of this, some people believe that dependence on nuclear energy will someday be unavoidable. Many others, however, insist that nuclear power must not be generated at all. This is because some of the waste created from nuclear energy is **radioactive**. Radioactive substances are extremely dangerous to human health, emitting tiny particles that can do great damage to all living cells.

In this radioactive waste storage facility in France, radiation from spent nuclear fuel gives off a blue glow. It has been estimated that spent nuclear fuel remains radioactive for more than 10,000 years.

Storing and disposing of nuclear waste is a major political and environmental problem, due to the threat it may cause to the well-being of future generations. When nuclear power was first being developed, the problem of what to do with radioactive waste was low on the agenda. However, it has now become an urgent priority as stocks of this waste continue to pile up. By the end of 1999, about 160,000 tons (145,000 t) of spent nuclear fuel was in temporary storage at nuclear sites worldwide.

High level nuclear waste can remain lethal for thousands of years.

Nuclear waste is categorized as High Level Waste (HLW), Intermediate Level Waste (ILW), or Low Level Waste (LLW). Of these three categories, LLW is the least harmful. Its radioactivity usually decays within a few months or years. HLW, on the other hand, has extremely high levels of radioactivity. It can remain lethal for thousands of years.

Although worldwide production of HLW is relatively small, safe disposal of this level of waste presents major challenges and concerns. HLW must first be stored for about 50 years before it has cooled enough to be transferred to a repository deep underground. Once underground, HLW must be kept isolated from the environment for approximately 10,000 years. The need for extreme isolation presents major challenges in HLW's management and disposal. Although constant efforts are made to improve the management of nuclear waste, it is very difficult to find long-term disposal sites for HLW. This is due mostly to public concern over the safety and reliability of proposed sites. There are even bigger storage and disposal problems related to the larger volumes of ILW, which may remain hazardous for hundreds of years. While engineers insist that technical storage and disposal solutions are available for ILW, the public remains unconvinced that long-term safety from the waste's radiation can be guaranteed.

There are more than 400 nuclear power plants throughout the world. As spent nuclear fuel continues to accumulate at these plants, solutions for safe, long-term storage become more and more pressing. The United States, with about 75 commercial nuclear sites, is expected to have more than 90,000 tons (85,000 t) of spent fuel by the 2030s. This amount is well above existing on-site storage capabilities. Today, governments in many countries are trying to find places to store nuclear waste permanently. Although plans have been made for long-term repositories in places such as Yucca Mountain, Nevada, and Sellafield, England, public opposition has delayed these potential disposal sites from gaining final government approval. As experts continue to work at ensuring the safety of possible repositories, nuclear waste continues to accumulate in storage facilities. Concern over nuclear material was heightened in early 2000 by a fire at a Japanese nuclear plant, a radiation leak at a power plant near New York City, and the forgery and **sabotage** of important documents at a reprocessing plant in Sellafield.

In 1986, an accident in Chernobyl, Ukraine, destroyed a nuclear reactor. Despite high levels of radioactivity present, most of the reactor's equipment has simply been dumped.

Hazardous Waste Manager

Duties: Develops, monitors, and evaluates hazardous waste programs to ensure compliance with government regulations
Education: Bachelor of science degree and often a master's degree in chemistry, biology, or environmental science
Interests: Protecting people and the environment

Navigate to the Environmental Careers Web site: www.eco.org for information on related careers. Also click on www.environmental-jobs.com for more information about hazardous waste jobs.

Careers in Focus

Hazardous waste managers are responsible for dealing with serious issues. They are in charge of developing programs and policies that protect the well-being of people who work with hazardous materials. They also make recommendations about how hazardous waste should be handled and stored.

Often in partnership with government organizations, hazardous waste managers inspect storage facilities, formulate regulations, and investigate accidents.

In the event of a hazardous waste accident, managers respond to the site to determine the best course of action. This usually involves assessing the amount of danger, taking samples of hazardous materials, and formulating a clean-up plan.

As much of their work is designed to protect the public, hazardous waste managers must be skilled communicators. They frequently address the media whenever concerns about hazardous waste arise. Hazardous waste managers must be able to remain calm in the face of confusion and fear.

Most hazardous waste managers begin their careers as hazardous waste technicians. They take samples from sites that contain hazardous waste and prepare them for laboratory analysis. After the material is tested, hazardous waste technicians develop reports and make recommendations to managers, who then assess the situation and decide what action to take.

The Landfill Option

There are three main ways for getting rid of waste: dumping, burning, and recycling. Dumping has always been the most popular method of disposal. Landfills are sites where waste has been dumped and buried. These sites are found in most countries around the world. Until the 1970s, most landfills were just crude, poorly covered garbage dumps, and very little thought was given to safety issues. This changed, however, when it was discovered that old landfill sites could leak harmful chemicals many years after they had been covered. Well-known incidents of such leaking occurred at Love Canal in the United States and at Lekkerkerk in the Netherlands, where old landfill sites had been sold for residential development. Toxic chemicals and gases seeped out of the ground at both sites, causing severe health problems for the people living in the newly constructed neighborhoods.

Modern landfills are carefully designed to protect against toxic leaks.

In 1980, concern over contamination from landfills led to the establishment of the

Superfund program in the United States. This program consisted of a $15 billion fund for the clean-up of dangerous landfills throughout the country. By the 1990s, thousands of contaminated sites had been identified across the U.S. Today, new sites are still being added to the list of those needing urgent attention. Many other countries, including England, France, Germany, and Japan have had similar problems with old landfill sites that leak toxins decades after being covered.

Public concern over poorly managed landfills led to many policy changes after the 1970s. In developed countries, strict regulations for the development of new landfills were put in place to ensure safe waste disposal. As a result, today's landfill sites are much different from the earlier unmanaged dumps. Modern sites are now carefully designed to protect against toxic leaks and to ensure the rapid biodegradation of waste. Many are also designed to tap energy from landfill gases, such as methane, and to provide useful fertilizer.

Although developed countries have made great improvements in landfill safety, the very existence of so many landfills points to another problem: the wastefulness of industrial society. People are producing so much waste that many countries are running out of landfill space. Some governments are now implementing strategies for reducing waste. For example, many countries force citizens and companies to pay a tax for garbage disposal in order to discourage the production of unnecessary waste. Several programs have also been established to promote waste-free thinking and to encourage more responsible forms of disposal. Ideas for waste reduction at home and at the office range from using smaller garbage cans to separating waste into different types so that some may be recycled.

Despite the use of plastic liners, clay layers, and **leachate** management systems, some experts claim that all landfills will eventually begin to leak. Whether such leaks are dangerous depends on the kinds of wastes in the landfill. If there are toxic wastes buried at the site, then leaking problems could be hazardous. Of course, it would be best if no toxic wastes were created in the first place. Unfortunately, toxic waste is part of the price industrial society pays for its own **consumerism**. Although it is unlikely that this consumerism will subside anytime soon, many people are beginning to realize that piling up waste is both inefficient and dangerous.

Along with the threat of leaking toxic wastes, landfills also emit potentially harmful gases. Rotting organic waste releases large amounts of methane and carbon dioxide, both of which are powerful greenhouse gases. These gases sit like a sheet of glass above Earth, trapping the Sun's heat and making the air warmer than usual. This increase in temperature is known as the greenhouse effect, and many scientists believe it is responsible for global warming. In many cases, methane produced at landfills is used as fuel, which makes better sense than allowing

The smoke emitted from the Payatas landfill in Manila, Philippines, is caused by a fire that burns within its center. This fire feeds off a continual supply of methane gas generated as the waste decomposes.

it to seep out into the atmosphere. However, carbon dioxide cannot be burned for fuel.

Some countries have better conditions for landfill sites than others do. In England, there are many old mine shafts and quarries that are suitable dumping grounds. Japan, by contrast, has very few suitable landfill sites, a fact that has led it to favor burning much of its waste. The United States, with its huge land area and geological **diversity**, has plenty of landfill sites, many of which are situated far from populated areas. The ability to situate landfills away from populated areas is more difficult in developing countries. In fact, there is a growing waste disposal problem in the developing world. Well-managed, sanitary landfills are still rare, and unofficial landfills remain quite common. In Manila, Philippines, as much as 40 percent of the country's daily waste output—6,600 tons (6,000 t)—is dumped outside of controlled landfills.

The United Kingdom contains about 4,000 landfills. More than 85 percent of all household waste in the UK is disposed of in landfills.

Although landfills cover up vast amounts of waste, the expression "out of sight, out of mind" is even more relevant when it comes to another form of dumping—marine disposal. The dumping of everyday waste from ships pollutes all the oceans. Added to this waste is the annual loss of about 165,000 tons (150,000 t) of fishing gear, including nylon fishing lines, buoys, and nets, all of which do not decay and can harm marine life. Plastic bottles, containers, and bags account for about 70 percent of the litter in the marine environment.

More harmful forms of waste have also been dumped into the world's oceans. For example, huge quantities of poisonous gas, chemicals, and weapons were dumped into the seas around Europe after World War I and World War II.

WHERE DOES IT ALL GO?

The world's biggest landfill is Fresh Kills, on Staten Island, New York. In the 1990s, Fresh Kills was taking in 13,000 tons (12,000 t) of municipal waste every day. The landfill was responsible for 5.7 percent of all methane gas emissions in the United States. As a result of environmental concerns, the landfill was closed in March 2001. The problem of how to deal with New York's waste has caused a great deal of controversy. The solution involves a mixture of recycling, incineration, and transport to new landfills in other areas.

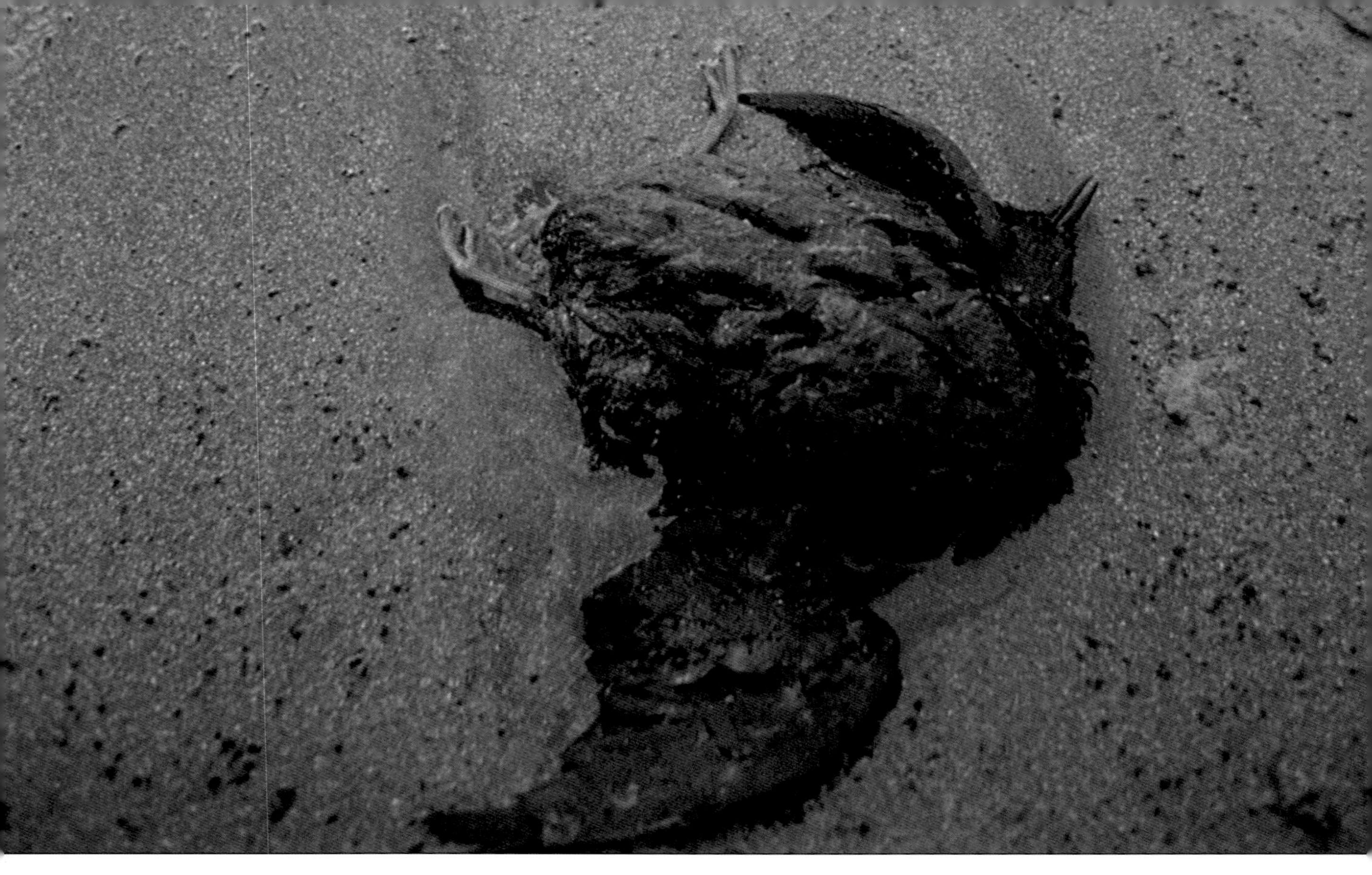

Even more alarming was the former Soviet military's routine dumping of radioactive waste in the Arctic and Pacific Oceans. This practice continued into the 1990s. Today, the Kola Peninsula in northern Russia has the world's largest concentration of nuclear reactors, and there is great international concern about radiation leaks when dumped nuclear waste containers eventually corrode at the bottom of the sea. Since 1972, the London Dumping Convention (LDC) has controlled international disposal at sea. Under the LDC, the dumping of hazardous and industrial wastes at sea is against international law. Despite this, marine disposal is still typical in many parts of the world.

On January 5, 1993, more than 25 million gallons (95 million L) of light crude oil spilled near the Shetland Islands, Scotland. The spill is the 12th largest on record.

KEY CONCEPTS

The modern landfill Today's sanitary landfills are sophisticated in design. They are also closely regulated. In a modern landfill, waste is spread in thin layers, each of which is compacted by a bulldozer before the next layer is spread. When about 10 feet of refuse has been laid down, it is covered by a thin layer of soil. This soil is also compacted, and then the landfill is closed. Many of today's landfills are divided into smaller units called cells. Only one cell of the landfill is open at a time, and it is covered nightly to reduce odors and pest problems.

The greenhouse effect Energy radiated by the Sun travels to Earth and warms the surface. Some of this energy becomes trapped in the atmosphere by gases, such as carbon dioxide. As a result, the lower portion of Earth's atmosphere experiences a rise in temperature. Most scientists acknowledge the greenhouse effect, but there is much debate about the causes and effects.

Waste Management Specialist

Duties: Supervises waste management facilities, conducts environmental assessments, assists authorities in responding to emergencies related to hazardous waste or materials

Education: Bachelor's degree in environmental science, and often a master of science degree

Interests: Environmental law, laboratory analysis, and safety procedures

Navigate to the Environmental Careers Web site: www.eco.org for information on related careers. Also click on www.environmental-jobs.com for more information about waste management jobs.

Careers in focus

Waste management specialists develop and review plans for the disposal of various kinds of waste. They are also responsible for ensuring that regulations for waste disposal are followed. Some waste management specialists focus on landfills, while others might be experts in chemical or hazardous waste.

Waste management specialists tend to have a broad base of experience in environmental planning and law. They must be knowledgeable about soils, hydrology, environmental monitoring, and waste treatment procedures. Waste management specialists rely on their research skills to help them formulate plans for the collection and interpretation of technical data. They use scientific methods to analyze situations and make recommendations for action.

In addition to an academic background in science, waste management specialists need strong communication and negotiation skills. They must be able to form solid working relationships with a variety of corporate executives and governmental organizations. Much of a waste management specialist's success hinges on his or her ability to communicate in a clear and professional manner. From writing technical reports to letters of inquiry, a waste management specialist must be able to develop effective communication strategies.

Waste management specialists usually work for municipal, state, or federal governments.

Waste Management Charts

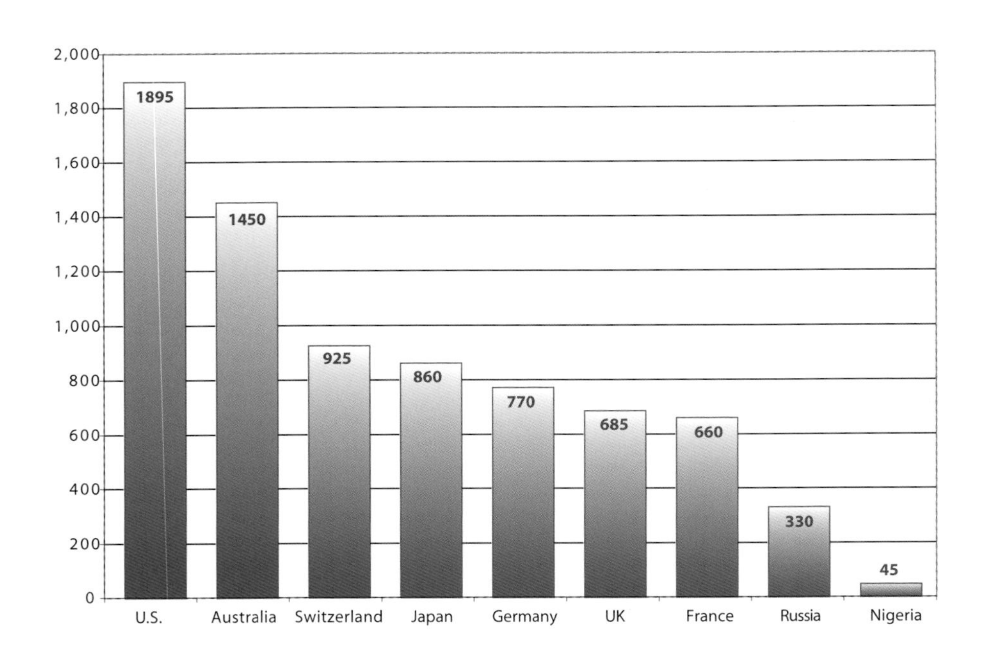

Figure 1: Municipal Solid Waste Generation

The U.S. leads the world in waste production, as shown in the chart to the left. Figures are in pounds per person per year.

Figure 2: U.S. Waste Disposal Practices

This chart illustrates the ways in which waste has been disposed of in the U.S. over time.

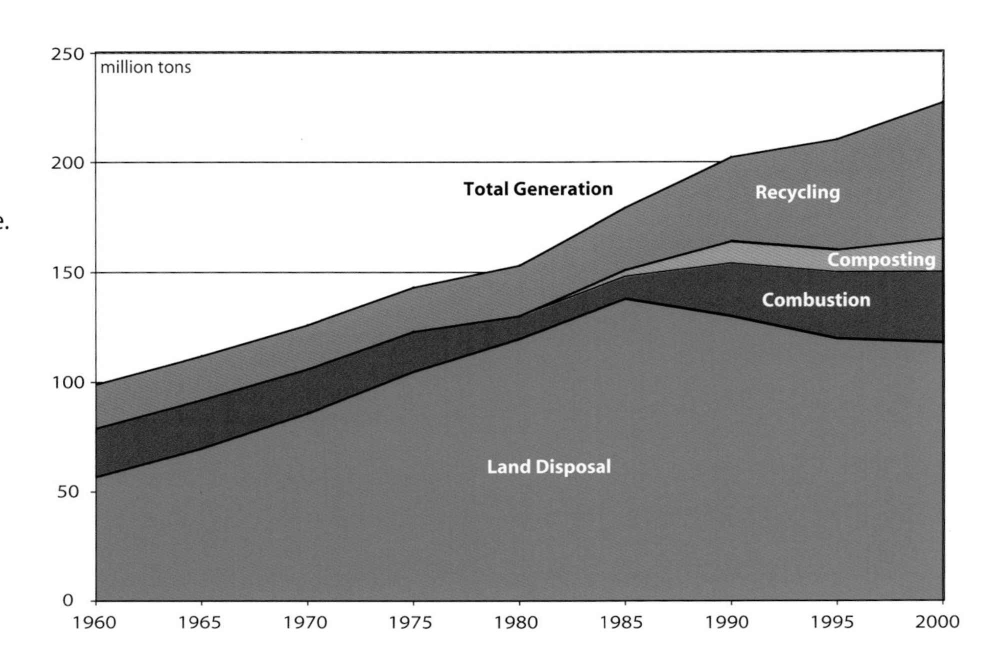

Figure 3: Traditional Industrial System

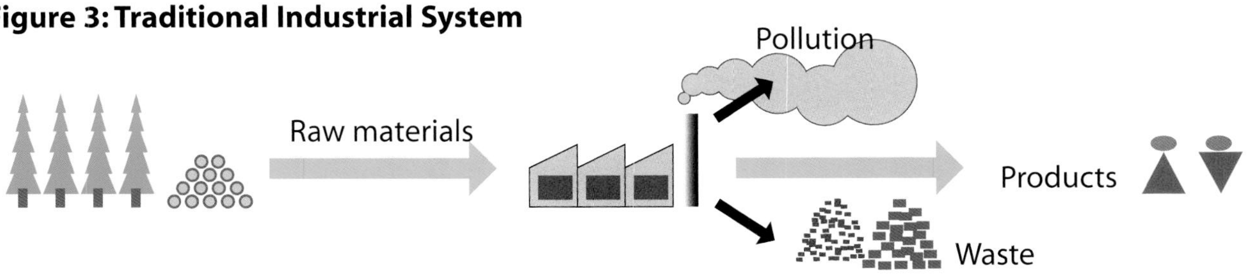

Pollution

Raw materials

Products

Waste

An unsustainable system, such as the example above, has serious consequences, including:

- Depletion of natural resources (especially non-renewable resources)
- Large-scale disturbance of soil and ecosystems
- Damage to human health

Figure 4: Zero Emission Industrial System (closed loop)

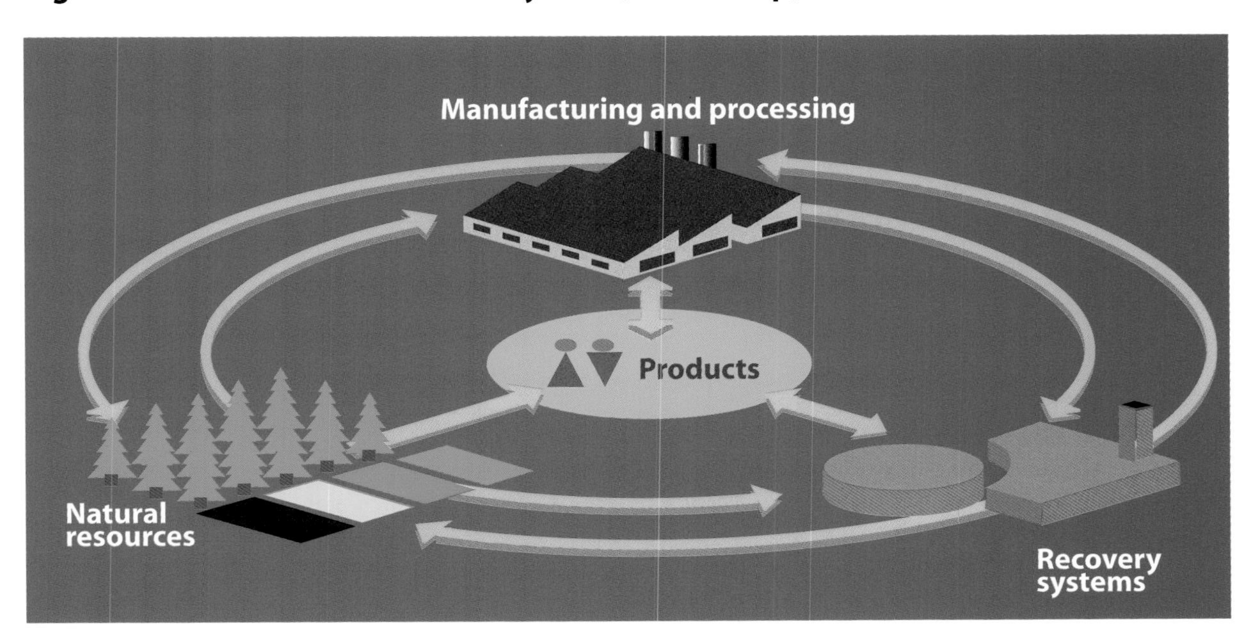

A sustainable system, as illustrated above, contributes to positive outcomes, including:

- Conservation of natural resources
- Better quality of life
- Protection of soil and ecosystems
- More jobs and higher profits

Handling the World's Waste

Figure 5: A Modern Landfill

Today's landfills are designed to minimize leaching and other environmental problems.

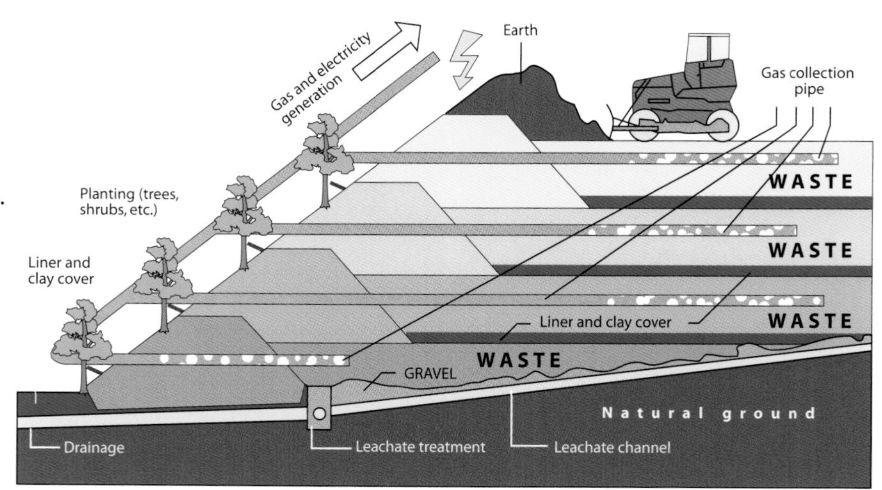

Figure 6: Treatment of Municipal Solid Waste

(Approximate figures, late 1990s)

The chart to the right shows measurements of total waste production. The chart also illustrates the ways in which different countries dispose of municipal solid waste.

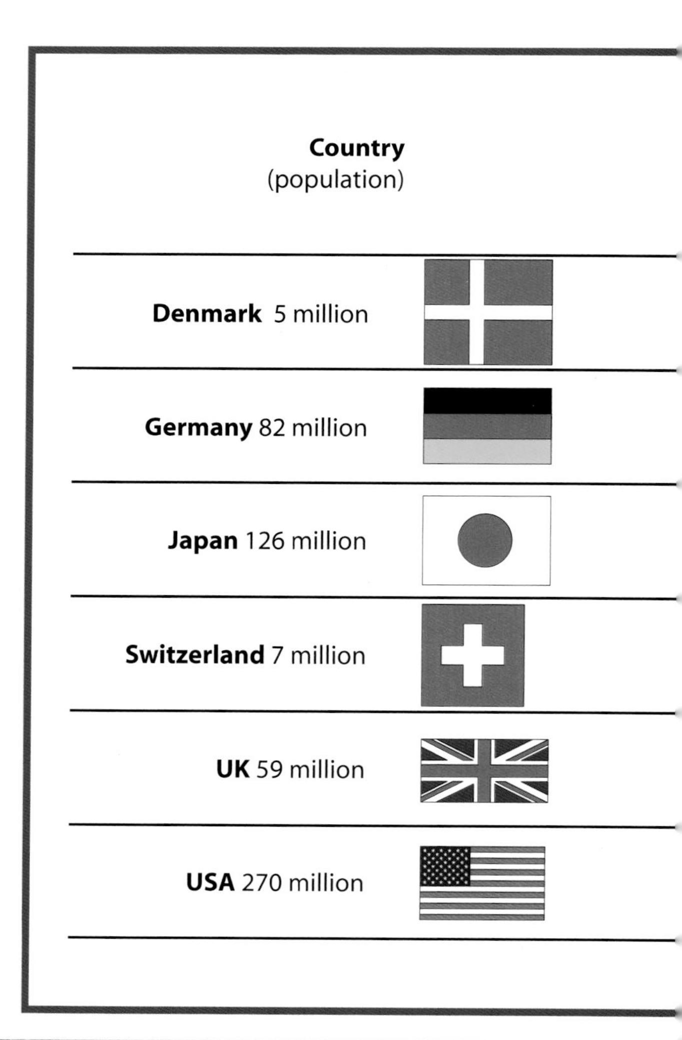

Country (population)
Denmark 5 million
Germany 82 million
Japan 126 million
Switzerland 7 million
UK 59 million
USA 270 million

Figure 7: A Modern Incinerator in Hamburg, Germany

Modern incinerators provide an alternative to landfills. Although the cost of incineration is high, the residue after burning is about 10 percent of the original volume.

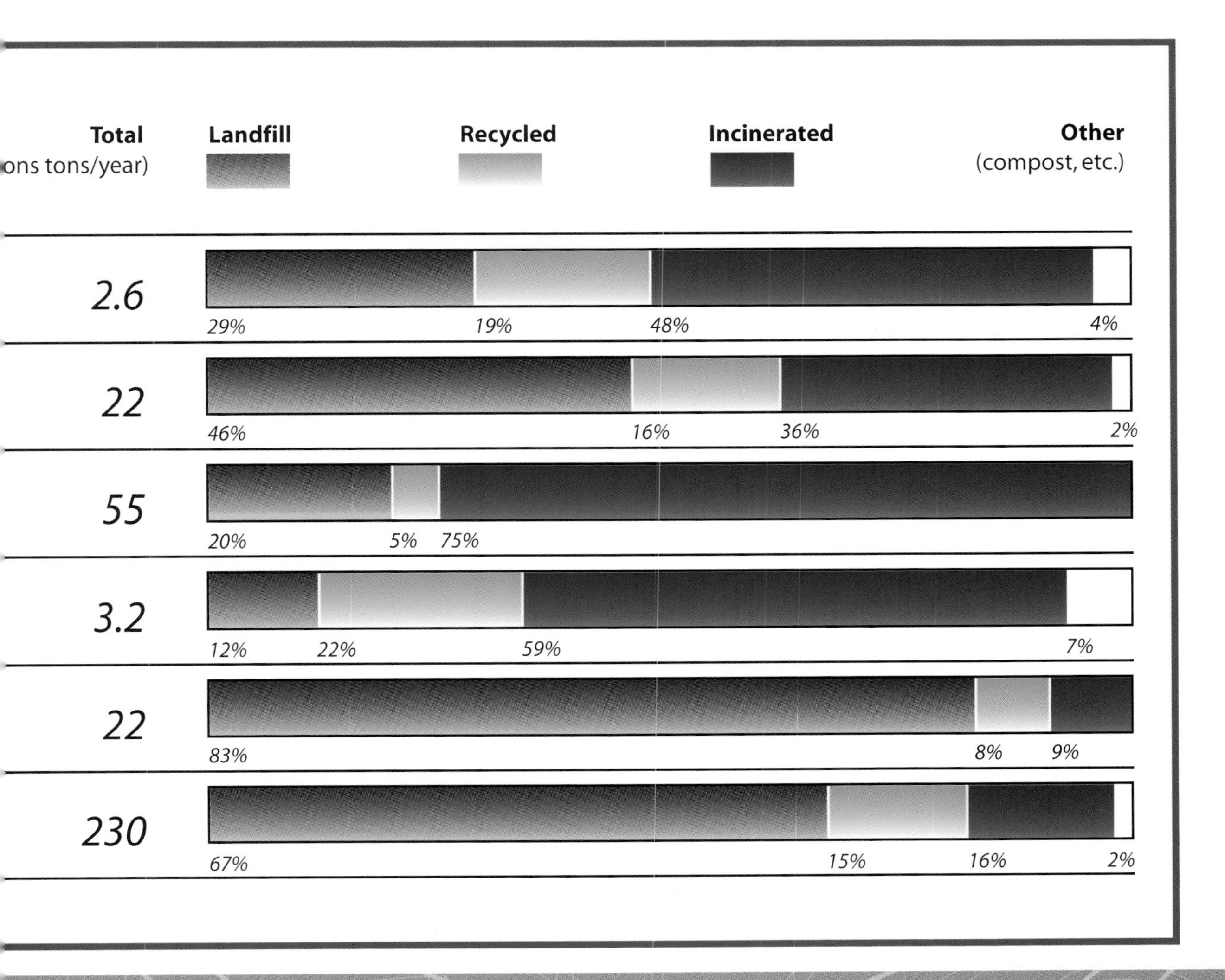

The Incineration Option

Incineration is another common solution for the removal of waste. In many ways, incineration presents a tidy solution to waste management. It can get rid of unsightly piles of garbage in very little time. However, incineration can also pollute the air with toxic emissions from burned matter. It is also known to destroy materials that could otherwise be reused or recycled. Years ago, incinerators were very basic, and they were used merely to reduce the volume of waste sent to landfills. At that time, little thought was given to the hazardous emissions that could be released during burning or to the amount of energy lost in the incineration process. By contrast, today's incinerating plants are designed to recover energy. These plants may be used to generate electricity, process heat for manufacturing, or provide hot water for heating systems. The burning of waste for energy is becoming more and more popular in many parts of the world. About 75 percent of Japan's municipal waste is incinerated, and in Europe, incineration is expected to account for 35 percent of municipal waste disposal by 2005.

More than 270 million used tires are discarded in North America every year.

Different kinds of waste release different levels of energy when they are burned. The **caloric** value of waste is the amount of energy it can emit during the incineration process. Old tires, for example, have a high caloric value. They can be burned for energy more effectively than other garbage such as food scraps or garden waste. Caloric values vary considerably. When burned, some wastes can be even more useful than coal or oil as a fuel. Items such as plastics, paper waste, and even chicken manure have high caloric values, providing rich sources of energy. Vegetable waste, however, has a relatively low caloric value, while glass bottles and metals have virtually none. Modern incinerators must be designed in relation to the types of wastes they will burn. As municipal solid waste (MSW) is made up of a great variety of substances, an incinerator for MSW will be designed differently than one specializing in old tires or plastic.

The burning of waste for energy is becoming popular in many parts of the world.

In order to reduce the danger of harmful emissions, a modern incinerator has to operate to very high environmental standards. Environmental laws in the developed world require incinerators to be fitted with a range of air pollution control devices. A modern incinerator will have sophisticated systems for removing harmful materials and scrubbing away acidic gases, such as sulfur dioxide and hydrogen chloride.

As a result of enforced safety requirements, running a modern high-temperature incinerator is both an expensive and demanding business. The incinerator's equipment must be able to withstand several demands, such as temperatures

CALORIE-WISE

Because some types of waste have such high caloric values, many people claim that burning garbage is an effective way to make energy. Those who oppose incineration argue that the amount of electrical energy produced is too small when compared to the amount of air pollution that burning creates.

of more than 1,800 °F (1,000 °C), continuous operation, and varying types and quantities of waste. The demands can often lead to problems such as the dirtying of pipes from gas deposits and the corrosion of tubes from contact with burning wastes. Huge amounts of dust are also generated by the burning process and must be controlled without being released into the atmosphere. As well, complicated precautions must be taken to ensure that escaping gases are harmless. These strict regulations have shut down all but the cleanest incinerators in the developed world.

Although modern incinerators follow strict guidelines, many people remain concerned about the harmful emissions that burning produces. It is often argued that a properly managed incinerator emits very few harmful substances.

However, some emissions are unavoidable and may contain a very fine dust known as PM10. PM10 particles are tiny, but they can be quite harmful to human health. Other airborne pollutants from incineration may include trace **heavy metals** as well as **dioxins** and **furans**. Though anti-pollution devices in incinerators may remove such pollutants, traces can also be found in the fly ash. This ash is produced during incineration and must be carefully managed. Most fly ash is collected within the incinerator and taken to a landfill. However, a small amount of ultra-fine ash may escape through the incinerator plant's chimney as part of exhaust gas.

Another problem with burning waste is that toxic emissions are not limited to the areas surrounding an incineration plant. Incinerator smokestacks are built tall so that exhaust gases are widely dispersed. The wind can end up carrying exhaust gases several miles away from the plant. Therefore, people living close to an incinerator may receive less **fallout** than people living downwind.

The Hundertwasser incinerator in Vienna, Austria, is equipped with two furnaces and is designed to burn 900 tons (820 t) of domestic waste per day.

HEAT SOURCES

Typical Caloric Values	Millions Btu/ton	GigaJoules/t
Fuel oil	36.1	42.0
Plastics	28.0	32.6
Tires	27.5	32.0
Coal	25.8	30.0
Dry sewage sludge	15.0	17.5
Paper	14.5	16.9
Industrial waste	12.9	15.0
Food waste	7.7	9.0
Municipal waste	7.3	8.5
Glass and metal	0	0

KEY CONCEPTS

Harmful emissions Although airborne pollutants emitted during the incineration process are minimal, they are believed to pose serious threats to human health. Among the most dangerous emissions are PM10s, trace heavy metals, and furans and dioxins. PM10s can cause damage to the human respiratory system. Emissions of trace heavy metals such as cadmium, chromium, and beryllium are also cause for concern because these metals are known cancer-causing agents. They can also cause neurological and pulmonary damage. While both PM10s and trace heavy metals are threatening, the worst pollutants produced in incineration processes are polychlorinated dibenzo dioxins and polychlorinated dibenzo furans. Better known as dioxins and furans, these two pollutants are among the most toxic of all chemicals. Even tiny amounts of dioxins and furans can cause death or serious health problems, such as muscular dysfunction, cancer, and birth defects.

PROS AND CONS OF INCINERATION

ADVANTAGES	DISADVANTAGES
Incinerators can be built close to the source of waste, whereas landfill sites must be located far away from populated areas.	The costs of incineration are high because of the need for advanced technology at the plant, wear and tear on equipment, and the sophisticated levels of operation required.
The residue of incineration is an ash that is only 10 percent of the volume of the original waste and about 30 percent of its weight. Inert ash may be used to supplement construction materials such as crushed stone or gravel, which are used to make cement.	There is a risk that reductions in operating standards could result in emissions that are dangerous to human health.
Incinerators can take a wide variety of waste and convert it to energy. Items such as tires, paper, food waste, plastics, chemical waste, sewage sludge, and chicken manure can all be burned for fuel.	The residue from incineration includes fine particles (fly ash) that may be contaminated with harmful pollutants.
Incineration can produce power for electricity, industrial processing, and district heating systems.	Incinerator performance may be affected by changes in the volume or makeup of waste burned. Continuous long-term supply of the same type of waste is ideal but often unachievable.
Incineration may be the most ecologically friendly option for disposing of certain hazardous wastes.	Incineration changes solid waste into gaseous waste that is much harder to control.
Incineration reduces the need for sanitary landfills.	Disposal of waste by incineration may lull people into believing that the waste problem has been solved and that no changes need to be made to wasteful lifestyles or industrial practices.

Biography: Gunter Pauli

Born: March 3, 1956, in Antwerp, Belgium
Education: Economics degree from St. Ignatius Loyola University, Belgium, master of business administration degree from INSEAD
Legacy: Founded the Zero Emissions Research Initiative (ZERI), which seeks to eliminate pollution in manufacturing

People in Focus

Gunter Pauli is an entrepreneur whose interests span science, business, culture, politics, and the environment. He has received worldwide recognition for his revolutionary business ideas.

After earning a degree in economics from St. Ignatius Loyola University in Antwerp, Belgium, Pauli went on to earn a master of business administration degree from INSEAD, a prestigious business school in France. After that, Pauli spent several years lecturing in Europe and performing consulting duties for IBM.

An accomplished entrepreneur and globetrotter, Pauli is perhaps best known for his work with the Zero Emissions Research Initiative (ZERI), which he founded. The ZERI Foundation was established on October 9, 1996, at the United Nations University in Tokyo, Japan. Its primary goal is the efficient production of all of the goods and services that the world needs—without any form of waste. In order to achieve this, ZERI has developed closed-loop manufacturing processes, where factories reuse or recycle all of the raw materials that they take in. Through redesigning systems of manufacture, ZERI has contributed strategies for worldwide sustainable development.

Among Pauli's other achievements are eight books, fluency in six languages, and numerous international awards. His records of entrepreneurial success and social consciousness make him a prime candidate for future Nobel Prizes.

Reduce, Repair, Reuse, and Recycle

In the first part of the 20th century, companies made products that were built to last. Customers regarded durability as a virtue, not because of concern over waste but because it was expensive to replace an item made by hand. As mass production by machines took hold, and materials such as plastic became available, consumer goods became less expensive. This made it easier for people to just throw things away. By the 1990s, U.S. citizens were throwing away 8 million television sets every year, along with 2 billion disposable razors, 18 billion disposable diapers, and more than 20 billion non-returnable bottles.

The invention of plastic is considered a major scientific achievement. Because of plastic, a variety of goods can be produced cheaply and in great quantities. Plastic has many advantages for manufacturers and consumers. It is strong, cheap, durable, and easy to shape. However, the production of countless plastic items has led to enormous problems in waste management. This is due to the fact that plastic is not biodegradable. In fact, it is nearly impossible to dispose of. Less than 20 percent of plastic is reused worldwide, and about another 20 percent is burned to produce energy. Recycling plastic is complicated and often results in a downgraded material that, though useful, does not have the qualities of the original plastic. In an effort to improve waste problems, the plastics industry is developing advanced techniques for recycling.

Since the 1990s, companies have been taking more responsibility for the goods they produce. Like plastics manufacturers, other major industrial companies are now considering the entire life cycle of the products they sell. Changes in law have made these companies responsible for health or environmental impacts at any stage in a product's life cycle, from raw-material collection to customer use and disposal. As a result, companies are aiming to reduce and recycle wastes that are generated by their products. Automobile manufacturers are focusing on designing new models with parts that can be recycled. They are also working toward reducing the impact of waste streams. Other companies are taking more responsibility by working together, using each other's waste material and surplus energy as input for different processes.

Recycling one ton (0.9 t) of cardboard saves more than nine cubic yards (6.9 cu m) of landfill space.

THE FIVE RULES OF ECO-EFFICIENCY

Every business has a responsibility to preserve natural resources and cut waste, pollution, and carbon dioxide emissions. Companies can be more eco-friendly by following these management policies:

1. Minimize the amount of material used in goods and services.

2. Minimize the energy used in providing goods and services.

3. Use renewable resources—material and energy—as much as possible.

4. Minimize toxic emissions.

5. Design durable products that can be repaired easily and use materials that can be recycled easily.

Recycling is an environmentally friendly way to manage many types of waste. One of the easiest materials to recycle is glass. Some bottles can simply be washed and reused. This is perhaps the most eco-friendly answer to glass waste because it saves 80 to 90 percent of the material and energy used to make new bottles. Old glass can also be ground up to form **cullet**, which can then be used to make new glass products. Since cullet melts at lower

temperatures than raw materials such as silica sand, recycled glass products are often cheaper than the original. Cullet can also be reused indefinitely. Glass recycling rates are high in many countries—at least 80 percent in Switzerland and 75 percent in Germany.

Recycling rates for paper are also quite high. Paper can be recycled about four times before its fibers break down into pieces that are too small for the manufacturing process to work properly. Paper recycling is important because it reduces the pressure on forests. After all, the manufacture of 1 ton (0.9 t) of new paper requires about 19 trees as well as large amounts of water, chemicals such as chlorine and sulfur, and high energy input. Though the pulp and paper industry is far more efficient than it used to be, global paper consumption is rising rapidly. Junk mail, one-sided photocopies, and 100-page weekend newspapers are just some examples of excessive paper use.

Paper recycling is important because it reduces the pressure on forests.

A variety of other materials can also be recycled or reused to help manage increasing levels of waste. Most countries have

It is estimated that only eight percent of waste is recycled in the UK. The British government aims to reuse 40 percent of waste produced by 2010.

systems for the recycling of scrap iron, steel, lead, copper, and zinc. In the United States, about 65 percent of pop cans are recycled, while both Japan and England recycle about 40 percent of their cans. Despite its mounting popularity, recycling is still considered to be an uneconomic venture in many countries. Recycling plants and collection methods can be expensive to maintain. To help with expenses, governments and other organizations in several developed countries provide funding for recycling businesses. Also, as more people are becoming aware of the world's growing waste levels, markets for recycled products are beginning to prosper. The Chicago Board of Trade, one of the world's main commodity exchanges, now runs a successful market in recyclables such as tires, plastics, glass, and paper. As well, the world's largest waste disposal company, the Houston-based Waste Management Inc., operates a Web site market for recyclable materials.

RECYCLING FACTS

Recycling 1 ton (0.9 t) of newspaper saves 19 trees.

Recycling one aluminum can saves enough energy to power a television for two hours.

It takes 95 percent less energy to recycle a can than it does to make a new one from raw materials.

A discarded glass bottle will take one million years to decompose.

It takes about two to three minutes per day to recycle.

Although recycling is now quite common, there are still many companies worldwide that manufacture non-recyclable disposable products. As well, there are still many customers who prefer the convenience that these disposable products may offer and who choose to ignore the wasteful consequences.

KEY CONCEPTS

Recycled products Recycling is one of today's most ecologically friendly ways of managing a variety of wastes. A great deal of society's everyday garbage is recycled into very useful goods. For example, newspaper and magazines are de-inked, pulped, and turned into newsprint again. Mixed paper and cardboard are processed into roof shingles, metal cans are melted down and made into reinforcement bars or wire mesh, and colored glass is used in making fiberglass insulation.

Renewable resources Many of Earth's resources are renewable—they can be replaced. Examples of renewable resources include solar, wind, hydroelectric, and geothermal power.

Toward Zero Emissions

Today, many companies have made it their goal to achieve total productivity. They are aiming to produce no waste, no defects, no inventory, and no pollution. This is known as zero waste, or zero emissions, and it means that traditional waste management is being re-oriented towards resource management. People have come to use the word *waste* to describe not only garbage but also the inefficient use of resources. Nothing demonstrates the wasteful use of resources quite like a car's use of energy. About 90 percent of the energy in a car's fuel is lost in wasted engine and exhaust heat—only 10 percent is used to power the vehicle. The motor industry is gradually changing in order to address this wastefulness. The next generation of motor vehicles will feature lightweight bodies, high fuel efficiency, and no polluting emissions.

The move to improve resource use and waste management is not limited to the automobile industry. Many other industries are looking at ways to reduce the environmental impact of their activities. The fuel industry itself is beginning to take a serious interest in renewable energy. Natural, renewable energy can be harnessed from the Sun, wind, or water. There are infinite supplies of renewable energy sources, and they do not produce waste or pollute the environment. As well, many companies are researching ways in which to use their waste as secondary material or fuel.

The fuel industry is beginning to take a serious interest in renewable energy sources.

Despite ongoing efforts to reduce waste levels, the volume of consumer items produced worldwide continues to increase. As a result, natural resources continue to be depleted, and waste volumes continue to grow. In the long term, the planet will not be able to support industrial society's current approach to production. In 1989, a program known as The Natural Step (TNS) was formed to provide guidelines for businesses that wanted to contribute to a sustainable society. Since the founding of TNS, large companies in Australia, England, Germany, Sweden, and the United States have embraced its strategies.

One of the best-known supporters of TNS is Interface, a U.S. carpet company that has transformed the office carpet business. With Interface, offices lease carpets instead of buying them. Interface takes responsibility for the whole life cycle of its carpeting, replacing and recycling worn carpet tiles as necessary. The system has greatly reduced the amount of carpet taken to landfills. It has also reduced the amount of disruption caused by the periodic replacement of carpet. As a result, service at Interface has improved, the environment has benefited, and the company has increased its profits. Imagine if all large companies adopted such responsibility for their products.

Companies are beginning to realize that reducing waste can lead to an increase in profits. In the 1990s, several large companies enjoyed significant increases in annual income because of their efforts to reduce waste. A recent report published by the World Business Council for Sustainable Development (WBCSD) describes how various high-profile companies have diminished waste production and are now enjoying the benefits. For example, since 1994, Xerox has achieved more

Utility-scale wind turbines are efficient providers of energy. They also contribute to a policy of zero emissions.

than 80 percent recycling of its products, as well as annual savings of $85 million through the recovery and reuse of old office equipment. The Canadian paper pulp manufacturer Millar Western is also enjoying greater success due to responsible production. It has developed a safe, chlorine-free process that can get 100 tons (90 t) of pulp from 110 tons (100 t) of wood, which is a yield 70 to 100 percent greater than traditional mills, without the usual pollution problems. Other papermaking companies are experimenting with different methods of production to reduce waste and increase efficiency. Because paper accounts for one-third of municipal waste, its impact is considerable. By 1999, more than 10 percent of the world's paper came from non-tree resources, and in China, the proportion reached as high as 60 percent. Paper can be made from sugar cane waste, elephant grass, hemp, canary grass, and straw.

In 1996, Gunter Pauli established the Zero Emissions Research Initiative (ZERI) to help diminish the waste levels produced by industrial processes. According to Pauli, world industry is only making use of 10 percent of the biomass of its raw materials. ZERI designs ways of creating more income and jobs from the same materials. An African brewery, for example, was shown how to grow mushrooms on grain waste, creating high-carbohydrate cattle feed while also producing earthworms, which serve as feed for a chicken farm. Methane from the farm animals is burned to provide energy for brewery operations. This kind of system, if applied to larger businesses, would allow companies to reduce waste by establishing beneficial relationships with other industries.

Many of the world's most powerful companies have not adopted a "zero emissions" approach. As it stands today, they do not have to account for their waste generation. Despite new landfill taxes, companies that produce large volumes of waste often pay no penalty, just as a citizen leaving 10 bags of

The U.S. pulp and paper industry consumes more than 12,000 square miles (31,000 sq km) of forest each year. About 40 percent of all trees logged are used for paper production.

THE NATURAL STEP

The Natural Step (TNS) was founded in 1989 by Karl-Henrik Robert, a Swedish doctor who was alarmed by the health risks associated with the world's increasing environmental problems.

He asked a panel of scientists to define the basic elements of a sustainable society. The result was the following four requirements: reducing dependence on non-renewable materials; phasing out non-biodegradable substances; protecting and maintaining the soil, the oceans, and biodiversity; and being fair and efficient in the use of natural resources.

Several large Swedish companies adopted these requirements as a guide to their management policy, and TNS has since spread to many large and small businesses worldwide.

garbage pays no more for its collection than a citizen with a single bag. There is no international requirement for companies to report the impact they make on the environment or to pay the cost of this impact. This must change if society wishes to sustain the environment. One way to help implement change is to support companies that use environmentally responsible production methods. When companies that support the environment are seen to have a competitive edge, others will follow their lead.

HOW YOU CAN HELP

You can help reduce the amount of waste produced by taking a few simple steps:

1. Recycle cans, bottles, and paper.
2. Turn household organic waste into compost.
3. Limit the amount of packaging you use—buy bulk refills whenever possible.
4. Buy products made from recycled materials.
5. When given the option, choose paper products over plastic ones.
6. Buy ethically—choose products made by companies that are committed to environmental preservation.

Time Line of Events

About 5,000 years ago

Ancient peoples in what is now Norway create a large garbage dump.

Around 500 B.C.

Greek and Roman civilizations develop advanced techniques of waste management, including elaborate sewage systems that bring in fresh water to wash the streets clean. In Athens, Greece, a law is passed that requires waste to be disposed of at least one mile (1.6 km) from the city.

A.D. 105

Paper is invented in China by Ts'ai Lun.

200

The city of Rome, Italy, creates the first sanitation force. Teams of two collect garbage and place it in a wagon.

1388

The British Parliament bans the dumping of waste in waterways and ditches.

1400

So much garbage is piled outside of Paris that it interferes with the defense of the city.

1690

The world's first paper-recycling mill is established near Philadelphia, Pennsylvania.

1776

Metal is recycled in the United States. Patriots melt down a statue of King George III and turn it into bullets.

1810

Peter Durand patents the tin can in London, England.

1885

The first garbage incinerator in the U.S. is built in New York State.

1898

New York City establishes the first recycling center.

1900

Recycling takes a twist as pigs are fed fresh garbage.

1904

Large-scale recycling begins in Chicago, Illinois, and Cleveland, Ohio.

1907

Leo Baekland, a New York chemist, invents "Bakelite," which becomes known as "plastic."

1912

Cellophane is invented by Jaques Brandenberger, a Swiss chemist.

1935

The first beer can is produced in Richmond, Virginia.

1943

Researchers at the U.S. Department of Agriculture invent the aerosol can.

1944

Styrofoam is invented by the Dow Chemical Company.

1948

Fresh Kills Landfill is opened on Staten Island, New York.

Mid-1950s

An outbreak of disease in piggeries prompts legislation requiring all garbage to be cooked before it is fed to pigs.

1965

The first solid waste management laws are passed in the U.S.

1970

The first Earth Day celebrations are held.

1970

The Environmental Protection Agency (EPA) is established in the U.S.

1974

Curbside recycling bins can be found in University City, Missouri.

1976

The Resource Conservation and Recovery Act is passed, requiring all garbage dumps to be replaced with "sanitary landfills."

1989

The Basel Convention is passed.

1990

McDonald's announces its intention to stop using polystyrene containers.

2001

Fresh Kills Landfill is closed.

Much of the waste that reaches landfills still has value. Many people in developing countries must resort to salvaging the goods that are discarded by others.

Concept Web

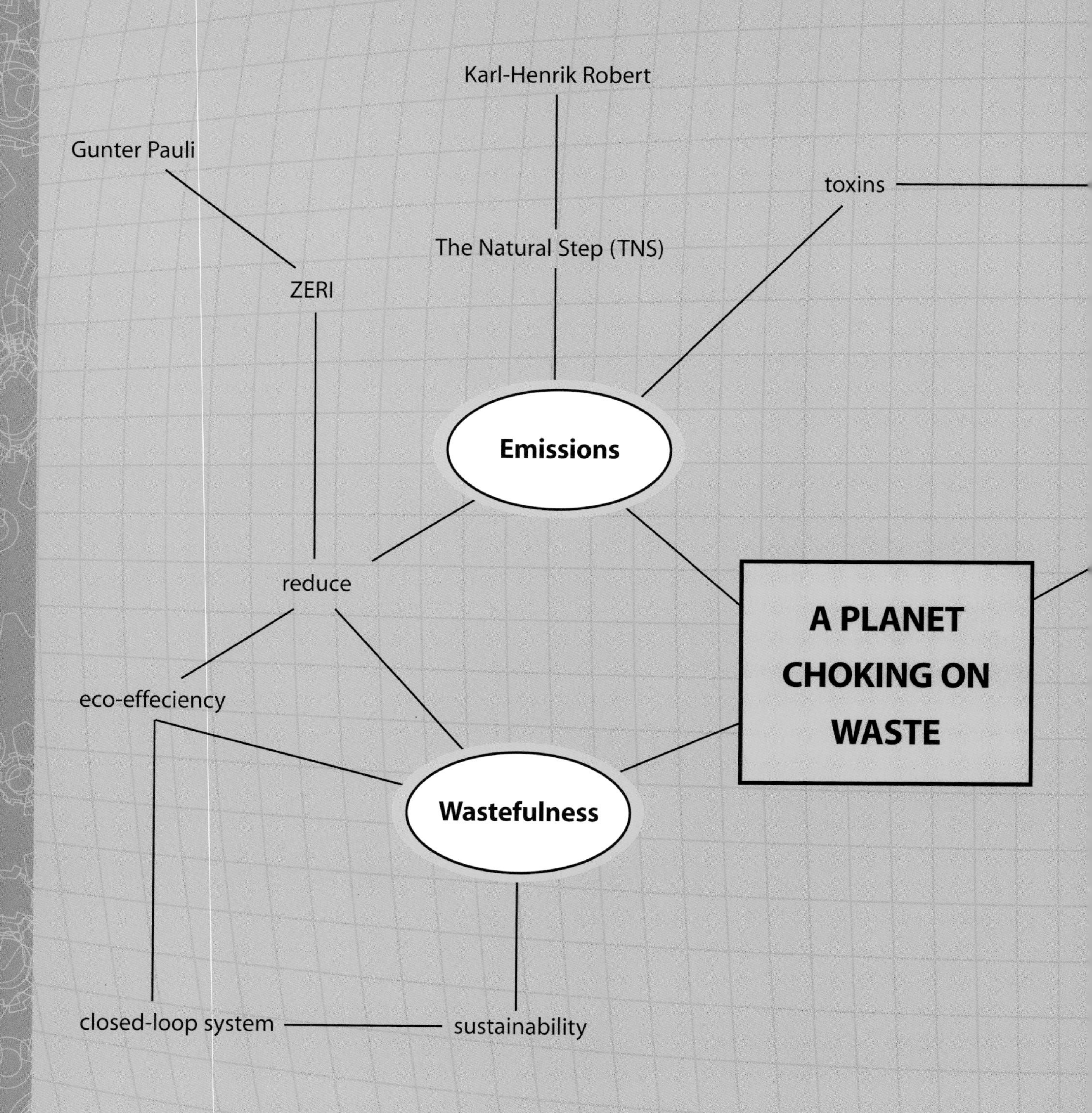
Karl-Henrik Robert
Gunter Pauli
toxins
The Natural Step (TNS)
ZERI
Emissions
reduce
A PLANET CHOKING ON WASTE
eco-effeciency
Wastefulness
closed-loop system
sustainability

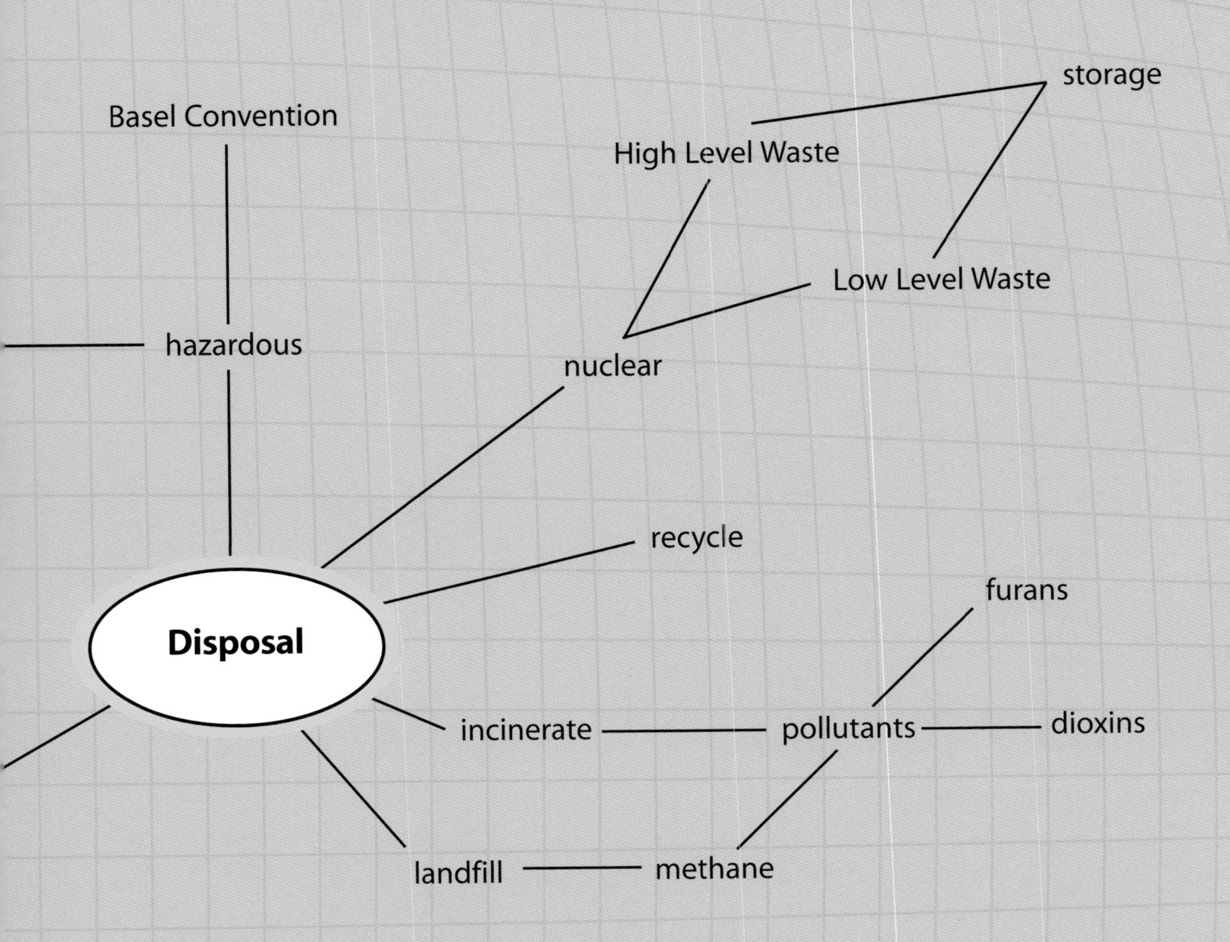

MAKE YOUR OWN CONCEPT WEB

A concept web is a useful summary tool. It can also be used to plan your research or help you write an essay or report. To make your own concept web, follow the steps below:

- You will need a large piece of unlined paper and a pencil.
- First, read through your source material, such as *A Planet Choking on Waste* in the Understanding Global Issues series.
- Write the main idea, or concept, in large letters in the center of the page.
- On a sheet of lined paper, jot down all words, phrases, or lists that you know are connected with the concept. Try to do this from memory.
- Look at your list. Can you group your words and phrases into certain topics or themes? Connect the different topics with lines to the center, or to other "branches."
- Critique your concept web. Ask questions about the material on your concept web: Does it all make sense? Are all the links shown? Could there be other ways of looking at it? Is anything missing?
- What more do you need to find out? Develop questions for those areas you are still unsure about or where information is missing. Use these questions as a basis for further research.

Quiz

True or False

1. Landfills are producers of methane gas.
2. Fresh Kills in Staten Island, New York, is one of the world's newest landfills.
3. Waste disposal has become a worldwide problem.
4. Gunter Pauli's organization seeks to eliminate emissions.
5. About 80 percent of a car's fuel-energy is wasted.

Multiple Choice

1. How long does a glass bottle take to decompose?
   a. one year
   b. 10 years
   c. 1,000 years
   d. one million years

2. What are the "three Rs"?
   a. Reinvent, retest, reproduce
   b. Reduce, reuse, recycle
   c. Revamp, rebuild, reuse
   d. Repeal, rewrite, retry

3. What percentage of waste is generated by the nuclear industry?
   a. 10 percent
   b. one percent
   c. 0.1 percent
   d. four percent

4. Modern landfills are:
   a. more dangerous than earlier ones.
   b. carefully designed and monitored.
   c. non-existent.
   d. too expensive to use.

5. Most waste is either:
   a. inert or putrescible.
   b. municipal or rural.
   c. chemical or nuclear.
   d. burned or fed to pigs.

Matching

Match a statement from the top with an answer from the bottom.

1. Environmental concerns prompted the closure of the world's largest landfill
2. A Stone Age garbage dump is discovered by scientists
3. Leo Baekland invents plastic
4. Homes were built on top of a landfill in this neighborhood
5. The world's largest concentration of nuclear reactors is here
6. These are among some of the most problematic pollutants
7. Presents international standards for the management of hazardous waste
8. Gunter Pauli's organization
9. About 75 percent of this country's municipal waste is incinerated
10. A rule of eco-efficiency

a) New York
b) Fresh Kills, Staten Island
c) Minimize toxic emissions
d) Kola Peninsula, Russia
e) Zero Emissions Research Initiative
f) Japan
g) Love Canal
h) Norway
i) POPs
j) Basel Convention

Answers on page 53

Internet Resources

The following organizations are devoted to waste management issues:

THE BASEL CONVENTION

http://www.basel.org

The Basel Convention provides international solutions for managing hazardous waste. This Web site outlines the details of the convention as well as its goals and achievements.

GLOBAL DIRECTORY FOR ENVIRONMENTAL TECHNOLOGY

http://www.eco-web.com

The Eco-web is a collection of articles and databases that relate to current environmental issues. From commentary by leading researchers to listings of environmental products, this site has excellent educational resources for people interested in environmental preservation.

UNITED NATIONS ENVIRONMENT PROGRAMME

http://www.unep.org

Established in 1972, the United Nations Environment Programme (UNEP) promotes sustainable development through responsible environmental practices.

Some Web sites stay current longer than others. To find other waste Web sites, enter terms such as "landfills," "incinerators," or "ZERI" into a search engine.

Further Reading

Ackerman, Frank. *Why Do We Recycle?* Washington, D.C.: Island Press, 1997.

Bagchi, Amalendu. *Design, Construction, and Monitoring of Sanitary Landfill.* New York: Wiley, 1990.

Bourgeois, Paulette. *Canadian Garbage Collectors.* Toronto: Kids Can Press, 1991.

Caldicott, Helen. *Nuclear Madness.* New York: Norton, 1994.

Cross, Michael. *Grow Your Own Energy.* Oxford: Blackwell, 1984.

Freeman, Harry M. *Incinerating Hazardous Wastes.* Lancaster, PA: Technomic, 1988.

Williams, Paul T. *Waste Treatment and Disposal.* New York: Wiley, 1998.

Answers

TRUE OR FALSE:

1.T 2.F 3.T 4.T 5.T

MULTIPLE CHOICE:

1.d) 2.b) 3.c) 4.b) 5.a)

MATCHING:

1.b) 2.h) 3.a) 4.g) 5.d) 6.i) 7.j) 8.e) 9.f) 10.c)

Glossary

biosphere: the parts of Earth and its atmosphere in which living things are found

byproducts: items produced when another substance is made

caloric: relating to heat transfer

closed-loop systems: systems in which the end product from the system is fed back into the system to create another end product

consumerism: the consumption of goods and services

cullet: broken or waste glass used to speed up the melting process in the manufacture of new glass

dioxins: toxic hydrocarbons

displacement: the movement of a substance from one area to another

diversity: variety

ecosystems: systems formed by the interaction of plants and animals with the environment

fallout: radioactive particles or dust that falls to Earth after a nuclear explosion

furans: colorless, flammable liquids

gangue: waste-rock and earth

heavy metals: metals, often toxic to organisms, which are very dense, such as lead, mercury, or copper

incinerators: furnaces or other facilities for burning garbage or other materials to ashes

inert: incapable of decaying

intensive: concentrated effort, usually in order to achieve something in a comparatively short time

leachate: the liquid produced in a landfill from the decomposition of waste

putrescible: capable of decaying or rotting

radioactive: emitting particles in the form of alpha, beta, or gamma rays as a result of the breaking up of atoms

sabotage: any damage or act of destruction intended to hinder or hurt

sludge: a soft, thick, muddy substance produced in sewage treatment processes

sustainable society: a group of people who have balanced environmental concerns with economics and the well-being of all community members

Index

Photo Credits

Cover: Landfill site (**Digital Vision**); **Title Page**: Fresh Kills Landfill, **Mark Edwards/Still Pictures**; **Kindra Clineff Photography**: page 27; **Corbis**: page 45; **CORBIS/MAGMA**: pages 8, 18 (**Roger Ressmayer**), 32 (**Craig Aurness**); **DigitalVision**: pages 2/3, 4, 6, 7, 9, 10, 12, 13, 14a, 20, 22, 25, 26, 40, 42, 47; **Tom Carroll/MaXx Images Inc.**: page 17; **Charles Shoffner/MaXx Images Inc.**: page 16; **PHOTO AGORA**: pages 14b (**Gerard Fritz**), 35 (**Jan Isachsen**), 15 (**Gary Mackey**),11(**Robert Maust**); **PhotoDisc**: page 21; **Hartmut Schwartzbach/Still Pictures**: page 31; **Jim Yuskavitch**: page 8; **Luis Guillermo Carmargo/ZERI**: page 37.